Technology

Cool Women Who Code

GIRLS IN SCIENCE

Andi Diehn

Illustrated by
Lena Chandhok

Nomad Press
A division of Nomad Communications
10 9 8 7 6 5 4 3 2 1

This book was manufactured by Marquis Book Printing,
Montmagny Québec, Canada
August 2015, Job #114418
ISBN Softcover: 978-1-61930-325-6
ISBN Hardcover: 978-1-61930-321-8

Illustrations by Lena Chandhok
Educational Consultant, Marla Conn

Questions regarding the ordering of this book should be addressed to
Nomad Press
2456 Christian St.
White River Junction, VT 05001
www.nomadpress.net

Printed in Canada.

~ Other Title in the **Girls in Science** Series ~

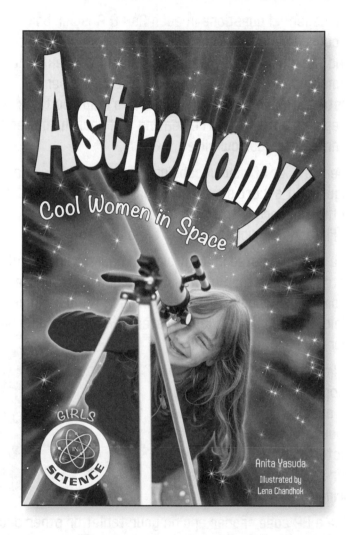

Check out more titles at www.nomadpress.net

HOW TO USE THIS BOOK

In this book you'll find a few different ways to further explore the topic of women in astronomy.

The essential questions in each Ask & Answer box encourage you to think further. You probably won't find the answers to these questions in the text, and sometimes there are no right or wrong answers! Instead, these questions are here to help you think more deeply about what you're reading and how the material connects to your own life.

There's a lot of new vocabulary in this book! Can you figure out a word's meaning from the paragraph? Look in the glossary in the back of the book to find the definitions of words you don't know.

Are you interested in what women have to say about astronomy? In the She Says boxes you'll find quotes from women who are professionals in the astronomy field. You can learn a lot by listening to people who have worked hard to succeed!

Primary sources come from people who were eyewitnesses to events. They might write about the event, take pictures, or record the event for radio or video. Why are primary sources important?

PS

Interested in primary sources?

Look for this icon.

Use a QR code reader app on your tablet or other device to find online primary sources. You can find a list of URLs on the Resources page. If the QR code doesn't work, try searching the Internet with the Keyword Prompts to find other helpful sources.

CONTENTS

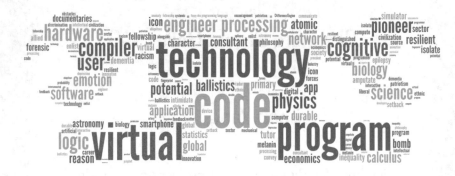

TECHNOLOGY IS EVERYWHERE

Technology is all around us. It's in our cars, our kitchens, and our bedrooms. We use technology when we play and work, at school, and to communicate with people around the world. We use it for entertainment, for education, and to save lives. Computers, smartphones, tablets, MP3 players, cars, artificial limbs, medical equipment, sports equipment—the list of things affected by technology is a very long one!

Ask & Answer

How does technology affect your life? What would your life be like without technology?

In *Technology: Cool Women Who Code*, you'll learn about three different women who work, or have worked, in the technology industry. These women faced many challenges as they made their way into the technology field, but they were determined to succeed.

Grace Hopper had a very long career in computers with the U.S. Navy. Shaundra Bryant Daily combines her passion for dance with teaching computer programming to her students. And Jean Yang is planning to be a professor of computer science.

 These women faced many challenges as they made their way into the technology field, but they were determined to succeed.

You'll read about their challenges, their inspirations, and their work. Maybe you'll be inspired! But first, let's look closely at some of the ways we use technology and discover the history behind the story of technology.

Chapter 1

TECHNOLOGY PAST AND PRESENT

Do you have a smartphone? An MP3 player for listening to music? Do you do your homework on a laptop? Technology may be all around us, but for many hundreds of years it looked very different. Technology is defined as the use of science to invent useful things or solve problems. When we use this definition, things that we might not think of as high-tech are actually considered technology!

A BYTE OF HISTORY

Today, we don't really think of fire as technology. But imagine living 350,000 years ago, when there were no heaters, fleece sweatshirts, or thermostats. What did people use to solve the challenge of staying warm and cooking food? Fire!

People didn't invent fire, they discovered it. But then they experimented with it until they could control it enough to use it to warm their caves and roast their meat. Fire is an early example of technology.

If you were making a list of technological tools, you might not think to include the wheel. But the wheel is actually one of the most important technological inventions in human history! So is the steam engine.

Without wheels and steam engines, our cities, roads, and entire civilizations would have never been built. How do we move heavy things over long distances? Wheels and steam engines are examples of humans using science to solve problems such as this.

 Without wheels and steam engines, our cities, roads, and entire civilizations would have never been built.

In the early 1800s, Charles Babbage wanted a better way to solve math problems. He used science to invent what is considered to be the first computer.

Babbage's Notebooks

Although Charles Babbage never had enough money to build either the Difference Engine or the Analytical

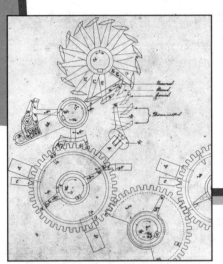

Engine, he made many drawings of how his machines would look and work. Do you find anything in this drawing familiar? Do you recognize these parts as belonging to a computer you'd see today?

Called the Difference Engine, his machine would be able to compute several sets of numbers. He later invented the Analytical Engine, which could do even more, including remembering the computations.

Unfortunately, Charles didn't have enough money to actually build his machines. He died without knowing if they would really work. It wasn't until the 1990s that a complete version of the Difference Engine was built for a museum.

Women were part of the computer industry when it was just starting in the early 1800s. Charles Babbage's friend, Ada Lovelace, worked on the Difference Engine and Analytical Engine with him. She wrote a series of instructions and articles about them.

Ada is considered a pioneer of programming. She was the one who suggested that computers could be used with words, not just numbers. This could make computers useful for a wide variety of jobs.

 Women were part of the computer industry when it was just starting in the early 1800s.

ADA LOVELACE

Ada Lovelace (1815–1852) was born to the famous poet Lord Byron and his wife, Annabella Milbanke. Annabella had studied math, which was very unusual for women back then. She decided her daughter should study math, too. Annabella didn't just think math was fascinating. She also wanted her daughter to be trained in something more practical than her father's poetry!

Ada met Charles Babbage when she was 17, and became interested in his ideas for a calculating machine. She later translated an article about the machine written by the Italian engineer Luigi Menabrea, to which she

The Turing machine, invented by Alan Turing in the 1930s, was another important step in the history of computers. It wasn't an actual machine. The Turing machine was the idea of a machine that could follow a series of steps using logic.

What made the Turing machine important was that it introduced a way for people to think about computer programming. Using the logic of the Turing machine, people could write instructions for computers.

A computer called the Bombe was partly based on the Turing machine. The Bombe helped the Allied forces break German codes during World War II.

dded lots of her own notes. Within those notes Ada escribed a logical series of steps to solve certain nathematical equations. Ada is considered the first omputer programmer. She is also sometimes called the rophet of computer science because she was the first ne to think about what computers might do beyond ath problems.

ou can view some of Ada's letters to Charles Babbage ere. What do you think it was like to be a oman working in technology at a time when at was extremely rare?

finding "Ada Lovelace" letters

Cool Career: Digital Musician

Digital musicians use computers to produce musical sounds instead of relying on individual instruments. When you see these artists, such as Holly Herndon, perform on stage, there are no bass guitars or harmonicas. There's just Holly standing behind a computer, making music.

Computers kept growing from there, both in size and capability. Companies began building computers that could calculate many lines of code, took up entire rooms, and cost millions of dollars.

These enormous machines were used by companies and the U.S. government. Families couldn't afford them and didn't have space in their homes.

 Today, many homes have a computer and often have more than one.

During the 1970s and 1980s, companies such as IBM and Hewlett-Packard began to produce computers that were more affordable and took up much less space. Many homes have a computer today, and often more than one. Most people carry smartphones in their pockets. Processing once took place very slowly on giant machines. Now it happens within seconds on tiny machines we hold in our hands.

CRACK THE CODE

Every piece of technology relies on computer programs and the people who code these programs.

A computer program is like a recipe. When you bake cookies, you use a recipe to make sure the cookies come out just right. You want them to be not too salty, not too hard, and not too gooey. You follow the instructions in your cookbook, measure the ingredients, and the cookies usually come out perfect, right?

A program is a list of instructions that tell a device what to do. A programmer codes the software so that when a user does something, such as click on an icon, the computer responds with the correct action, such as opening the right app.

There are many different languages for coding. Java, C, C++, Pascal, JavaScript, COBOL, BASIC, and Scratch are all programming languages.

Programmers use Java, C, and C++ to write programs that have to run very fast and do large amounts of work. JavaScript might be used to make games that run on web pages. Programs written in COBOL are found in many government computers. Pascal, BASIC, and Scratch are often used as teaching languages.

To learn to code, you need to think logically and think ahead. You need to think in sentences that follow the pattern, "If this, then that." Computers can't make guesses, so you have to tell them every single step.

When you follow a recipe to make cookies, the recipe might not say, "Reach out and turn the oven dial five clicks to the left." Usually it will say, "Heat the oven," and trust the cook to know how. Computers, however, need to be told every single step.

WHO'S BEHIND THE TECHNOLOGY?

Technology is so prevalent that it's easy to forget about the millions of hours people have worked to make technology available to everyone. Who are these people? Who's working all these hours and making all these devices? Well, different people all around the world. Let's consider smartphones.

First, someone had to have the idea for a computer you carry in your pocket. Someone else thought about combining that computer with a cell phone. Someone else said, "How about a camera?"

Another person suggested creating applications, or apps, for doing different things. These apps include checking the weather, reading ebooks, and looking at photographs shared by friends.

Logic? Logic!

Have you ever been described as a logical person? Has anyone ever sighed and said, "Oh, won't you be logical about this?" Logic is the study of the correct form of reason. We use logic to know that if all students are happy, and Samantha is a student, then Samantha is happy. Or, if X is less than 10, and Y is less than X, then Y is less than 10.

When a computer programmer codes, she uses logic to tell the computer what to do. She tries to think about all the different rules a computer will have to consider when trying to run a program. Learning to think logically is an important step in learning to program computers.

Then someone had to design the outside of this tiny computer. It had to be comfortable to hold to your ear, easy to stick in your pocket, and large enough to read the words on its screen.

A smartphone also had to be durable, because people drop things a lot! It had to be quiet enough to use in a crowded subway, but loud enough so its owner could hear when it rang. Or, hey, what if it vibrated when a call came in? Hmmm . . . .

There are lots of jobs in technology. Do you like figuring things out? Do you enjoy puzzles or riddles?

There are a few different kinds of jobs in technology. If you are interested in how things work, technology might be a good industry for you. Some people design hardware such as smartphones, artificial limbs, or medical tools. These are mechanical engineers who consider the size, shape, and design of different devices.

 Are you interested in how things work? Technology might be a good industry for you.

Civil engineers use technology to look at hardware on a very large scale, such as buildings, roads, bridges, and dams. Software developers think about how people, or users, interact with the information on their screens.

Programmers take ideas and turn them into real experiences. They code programs that allow users to see, touch, and listen. Programming is the kind of job that touches all areas of the technology industry.

Ask & Answer

Computers used to be huge and now they can be very small. What effect does the size of computers have on their availability? Why?

Language Lesson

Rear Admiral Grace Hopper was on the team that first developed the programming language called COBOL. She believed that computers should be accessible to everyone, not just mathematicians, so she worked on creating a language that uses words instead of just numbers. You'll learn more about her in Chapter 1. Here's an example of some COBOL programming. Can you tell what this code is telling the computer to do?

```
IDENTIFICATION DIVISION.
        PROGRAM-ID.
        HELLO-WORLD.
PROCEDURE DIVISION.
        DISPLAY 'Hello, world!'.
STOP RUN.
```

You might have heard about people who quit school and still managed to make it big in technology. Steve Jobs dropped out of college, and look how successful he was! People such as that, though, are anomalies. They're unusual!

Most people study hard and graduate from college before working full time in technology. In addition to computer and programming classes, technology students might take classes in math, science, engineering, art, and logic.

Technology of the Past

Today, photographs are everywhere. People snap pictures with their phones and share them easily on social media.

When Eadweard Muybridge used high-speed, stop-motion photography in 1878, it was a new technology of the time. This new technology allowed him to make a series of photographs of a galloping horse. He proved that, yes, all four of the horse's feet were off the ground for a split second during a gallop. He solved a major mystery!

In 2006, a piece of animation was made using Muybridge's photographs from more than 100 years before. You can see the animation here.

"Eadweard Muybridge" horse animation

"The Analytical Engine weaves algebraic patterns, just as the Jacquard loom weaves flowers and leaves."

—Ada Lovelace, early computer scientist

COMPUTING WOMEN

In 1985, 37 percent of computer science graduates in the United States were women. In 2012, only 18 percent of these graduates were women. This means that for every 100 computer science graduates, 82 are men and 18 are women. Does it matter if more boys than girls are shaping the technology industry?

Researchers have noticed that 1985 was the year computers became much more common in homes. For a long time, computers were marketed to boys more than girls. Like toy trucks, computers became known as boy things, not girl things.

 Does it matter if more boys than girls are shaping the technology industry?

All types of people use technology. Men, women, and people of all ages use technology. People in every country and people of every race, religion, and ethnic background use technology. If all these people use technology, doesn't it make sense that all these people contribute ideas about what this technology looks like and how it behaves?

Technology Team

The National Center for Women & Information Technology (NCWIT) is a nonprofit group that works to bring more women into the professional field of technology. They encourage girls of all ages, from kindergarten all the way through graduate school, to focus on computers and technology. NCWIT offers support to schools and professional groups that are making women in technology a focus. You can learn more about their work at their website: www.ncwit.org.

The U.S. Bureau of Labor Statistics believes that information technology is one of the fastest-growing industries. By 2020, nearly 1.4 million new jobs will have been added to the profession. Women make up more than half the working population in the United States, so it makes sense to train them for the jobs that need to be filled.

Ask & Answer

What will the computer industry be like 20 or 30 years from now if one gender continues to work in it the most?

This is an exciting time to learn about technology! Whether you join the profession or simply want to know more about the digital experience, you'll find exciting stories in these pages.

Follow Grace Hopper, Shaundra Bryant Daily, and Jean Yang on their journeys through the complex world of technology! These are women who have worked hard in a field dominated by men to succeed in ways they only dreamed about as girls. Their stories will inspire you to dream big.

Try It!

Technology is convenient. You can be working and playing with hardware, software, and programming before ever getting your dream job. In fact, you can start now! Check out these websites that are designed to teach people to start to think about how technology works, and even how to code.

hourofcode.com
scratch.mit.edu
madewithcode.com
lightbot.com
codecademy.com

Chapter 2

GRACE HOPPER

What if you were a girl in the early 1900s who liked math and science? Would your family and teachers encourage you to go to college to study these subjects? Most girls who lived during this time were told that they should concentrate on getting married and having children.

Some girls studied home economics, such as cooking and sewing, so they could better take care of a household. Grace Hopper had other ideas, though. And she was lucky to have parents who thought an education was a vital thing for a girl to have.

TICK TOCK, WHAT'S INSIDE?

Grace was born in New York City in 1906, the oldest of three children. She showed lots of curiosity as a young child. Her parents, Mary Campbell Van Horne and Walter Fletcher Murray, encouraged all of their children to have plenty of ideas and to think for themselves.

RACHEL RAMSAY

Rachel Ramsay is a graphic designer and faculty member at Dixie State University in the computer information technology department. When Rachel was 10 years old, she wanted more than anything to be an astronaut. Her fifth-grade teacher told her that she'd never be sent into space. That one comment dashed her dreams. As she grew older, Rachel realized that she wanted the girls she knew to be encouraged to pursue their dreams. It shouldn't matter whether those were dreams of becoming a dancer, venturing into space, creating art, being a scientist—whatever!

As a graphic designer, Rachel uses technology to create digital art. As a teacher, she noticed that there were fewer women than men in her classes. So she started a

Do you have any skills or interests that you might turn into a career?

Sometimes kids show early signs of what they're going to be when they grow up. If you spend lots of time balancing on your head, maybe you'll be a gymnast. If you are the one making dinner every night, perhaps you'll be a chef.

program for girls interested in technology called Girls Go Digital! It provides a place for girls to learn how to design, code, and make their own gadgets and devices.

Rachel says, "I believe that by inviting girls to become more involved in computer science and technology at an early age through fun and interactive projects, girls will become more engaged. Also it's important to see someone you can relate to doing something you're interested in."

Girls ages 8 to 18 join together at a yearly camp to delve into a subject they're all fascinated with—technology! You can learn more about Girls Go Digital! here.

— "Rachel Ramsay" girls go digital 🔍

Grace liked to understand how things worked. When she was seven years old, she decided to figure out how alarm clocks operate. She took apart the alarm clock that woke her up every morning and discovered a new world of springs, gears, and cogs inside. But she couldn't figure out how to put the clock back together. So she took apart another clock in another room.

Five alarm clocks later, Grace still didn't know how they worked. When her mother found the path of alarm clock destruction, she put a stop to it. However, Grace's mom did let her keep one of the clocks to keep experimenting on. Grace's parents wanted to encourage all their children to pursue their interests and to figure out how the world worked.

As an adult, Grace spoke of this incident with the clocks as an early sign of her attraction to technology. Of course, there were no household computers in Grace's childhood home, because they hadn't been invented yet!

> Grace's parents wanted to encourage all their children to pursue their interests and to figure out how the world worked.

Have you ever taken apart a computer or a toaster or an alarm clock? It's pretty fascinating to find out what's happening inside the case, isn't it? Grace certainly thought so.

AHOY, SAILOR!

Grace was always known as a resilient, determined person. These qualities later helped her at work when she was faced with difficult projects. She never gave up on tough problems that seemed impossible to solve.

When she was a young girl, she was out sailing alone on a lake when a sharp wind tipped her small boat over and spilled her into the water. Some children might have panicked and needed to be rescued. But for Grace, her mother's call from the front porch was enough. "Remember your great-grandfather, the admiral," Mary called calmly to her oldest daughter.

And that was exactly what Grace needed to be able to right her boat and get to shore. Her great-grandfather had been a naval officer during the Civil War. He had made a strong impression on Grace the one time she met him before his death. Later, she followed his footsteps into the Navy.

Ask & Answer

Have you ever been in a dangerous situation that you saved yourself from? What did you learn from the experience?

EARLY INTELLECT

Grace's parents encouraged their children to be curious, to read, and to talk about their ideas. Their house was filled with books and their dinner table was filled with conversation.

Her father, Walter, was an insurance agent. He suffered from such poor health that his legs had to be amputated because of problems with his arteries. This forced Grace's mother, Mary, to take over many of the household tasks that were generally left to men at that time. Mary was determined that her daughters would go to college.

Family Dinners

Does your family have dinner together? Grace's family encouraged lots of conversation at the dinner table. Recent studies have shown that Grace's parents were doing the right thing. Regular family mealtimes increase kids' exposure to healthy food, raise academic grades, and lower the number of instances of drug use among adolescents. Family mealtimes have also been shown to result in greater emotional well-being in children and parents. That's a lot of benefit coming from family dinners! And the dinner table is one place where it might be better to stay low-tech. No smartphones!

" . . . when we're in game worlds, I believe that many of us become the best version of ourselves, the most likely to help at a moment's notice, the most likely to stick with a problem as long at it takes, to get up after failure and try again."

—Jane McGonigal,
video game developer

Walter, too, thought college for his daughters was a good idea. He worried about his poor health and he wanted his family members to be able to take care of themselves in case he died young. Luckily, he lived a very long time.

The family went on many educational outings to museums, concerts, and historical sites. They also spent much of every summer at the family's summer home on Lake Wentworth in New Hampshire. This is where Grace and her siblings learned to swim and sail, as well as grow a vegetable garden, sew, cook, and work with tools. Grace spent a lot of summer afternoons reading books, too.

 Both of Grace's parents wanted Grace and her sisters to go to college.

Grace went to school at a private girls' school, as was the custom for wealthy families in the early twentieth century. When one of her cousins graduated from Vassar College, it was assumed by Grace and her family that she'd go to Vassar, too.

OFF TO COLLEGE

When it was time for Grace to go to college, she was required to take several entrance exams. Being a smart person, she expected to pass all of them without any problem. But something terrible happened—Grace failed her entrance exam in Latin.

JANE MCGONIGAL

Do you like to play video games? Has anyone ever told you that video games are a waste of time?

Jane McGonigal disagrees. She thinks video games are the solution to many of today's problems. Jane studied English and performance art and had begun developing video games when an injury caused a really bad concussion.

She was getting up from the floor in a hurry when she hit her head—hard!—on an open cabinet door above her. She suffered from nausea, dizziness, and memory loss, and she didn't feel better even after a whole month.

To help herself get better, she designed a video game she called *Jane the Concussion Slayer*, which has been renamed *SuperBetter*. She set one epic goal for herself, and then she set several smaller goals that were easier to achieve. She believes her game was an important part of her recovery.

Failing Latin meant she couldn't go to college. She was very disappointed in herself, but that didn't mean she gave up and stayed home. Instead, Grace went to a girls' boarding school in New Jersey called the Hartridge School for a year, preparing herself for the start of college. She had suffered a setback, but that didn't stop her.

Jane thinks that the energy people put into solving the problems they encounter in video games can be put to use solving real-world problems, such as environmental concerns. That's what she did with *Jane the Concussion Slayer*.

She says in a TED talk, "…there's no unemployment in *World of Warcraft*. There is no sitting around wringing your hands, there's always something specific and important to be done. And there are also tons of collaborators. Everywhere you go, hundreds of thousands of people are ready to work with you to achieve your epic mission."

She thinks that this level of collaboration is essential to tackling the major issues that face our civilization, and that the more we play collaborative video games, the better we'll get at solving those issues.

Watch Jane get people to connect with each other with *Massively Multi-player Thumb Wrestling*.

"Jane McGonigal" TED talk thumb wrestling 🔍

Vassar College had been originally established to provide women with a solid foundation of academic study. But during the Great Depression and after World War II, it began to offer more classes that prepared its students for marriage and motherhood.

Women's Rights

When Grace was a girl, women didn't have the right to vote. This meant only men had a say in who became the elected leaders of the United States. The right to vote wasn't established for women at the national level until 1920, though some states and smaller regions made it legal before this. Can you imagine what it would be like if women still couldn't vote? What might be different in our country?

Even though women gained the right to vote nearly 100 years ago, we still haven't had a female president of the United States. We do have many women serving in Congress and in the White House, and currently three women serve as justices on the Supreme Court. There have been female governors and mayors and many women serve in other offices in state government. Do you think a woman will become president in your lifetime?

TECHNOLOGY

Classes with titles such as "Husband and Wife" and "Motherhood" began to gain popularity. This switch was partly because, during the Depression, people thought women should let men have the few jobs that existed.

Then, after World War II, there were many returning soldiers who needed jobs. Society decided women should take care of their homes and families instead of working at businesses.

Ask & Answer

How does society's opinions affect you? If society thought you should only have a certain type of job, would you follow that suggestion?

Grace rejected the notion that women should stay at home. She got into Vassar and studied math and physics, the science of forces and matter. It didn't occur to her to follow conventions and study subjects that would have left her qualified to work only in her own home.

Not only did Grace work hard at her own subjects, she also helped other students in their classes. When the daughter of one of the college's trustees was failing, Grace stepped in as her tutor.

Grace soon gained a reputation for being a great teacher. She thought that experimenting was the best way to learn something. Have you ever sat in science class and listened to your teacher talk about something that makes no sense? But then you perform an experiment that shows you what your teacher has been talking about and suddenly it all becomes clear?

Grace showed her students what she was teaching them. Her demonstrations included having a student step into a full bathtub when she was teaching about displacement. When her students saw the water spill over the edge of the tub, they could see displacement for themselves.

Move Over, Matter

Displacement is what happens when one body of matter, the student, takes up space in another body of matter, the water. Two bodies of matter can't take up the same space at the same time, so some of the matter has to shift.

An ancient Greek physicist named Archimedes (c. 287 BCE–c. 212 BCE) discovered that the amount of matter that moves over is equal to the amount of matter added. The legend goes that Archimedes was getting into his bathtub when he made this discovery, which is called Archimedes' principle.

After Grace graduated from Vassar, she won the chance to study math at Yale. She got her master's degree and started a PhD program in 1930. This is the most advanced degree in a subject. That same year, she married a man named Vincent Hopper, who taught literature at New York University's School of Commerce.

Grace kept teaching while she studied and wrote her dissertation. This is a long essay that is part of the requirements of a PhD. As a teacher, Grace showed the same habit of innovation that she would later use when working with computers. She did more than just teach about a subject. She thought about how to best convey the information to her students so that they felt the same level of passion for a topic that she felt for it.

 Later, Grace showed the same habit of innovation with computers.

One way she did this was to have her students listen to her lecture and then write it up from their notes. Grace then read their notes and gave them feedback.

Some students complained about this. They figured that since they were taking a math course, they shouldn't be writing so much. Grace disagreed. She pointed out that being able to communicate clearly was an important skill in all subjects.

Grace was willing to teach subjects she wasn't an expert in. There were many times that she learned new material just before she had to convey it to her students in class.

When Grace agreed to teach a course in a math subject called finite differences, for example, she knew nothing about it. She'd only had one semester of probability when she took that on, too. Later, Grace found that she used the knowledge she gained teaching these courses in her work with computers.

Cool Career: Security

Have you ever ordered a book from Amazon? People around the world put their personal information, including credit card numbers, on the Internet. There is always a danger that someone else will figure out how to access that information and use it illegally. People working in security try to make sure that doesn't happen by designing safety processes and software, testing companies for security holes, and trying to anticipate crimes before they happen.

Probability? Probably!

Let's say you flip a coin 20 times in a row. If it comes up heads every time, what are the chances the next flip will come up tails?

Every time you toss a coin, probability dictates that there is a 50-50 chance the coin will come up tails. This means there is also a 50-50 chance the coin will come up heads.

Probability is the study of how likely it is that an event will happen. It is related to problem solving, which is what programmers spend a lot of time doing. Probability is important in computer programming. Computer scientists also use probability to determine how likely it is that a program will succeed.

Grace was interested in lots of different areas. She took courses in astronomy, philosophy, and biology even though they didn't count toward her degrees.

In her work with computer languages, she felt that the exposure to many different subjects was a great help. She was able to see how computers could be useful in all fields in all sorts of ways. Grace was one of the first people to understand that computers were more than calculators!

 Grace found that she used the knowledge she gained teaching different courses in her work with computers.

Grace was the first woman in Yale's 233-year history to earn a doctorate in math. After completing her degree, she kept on teaching. Why? Because she was very good at it. And it was one of the few professions open to women in the 1930s and 1940s. While she was teaching at her old college, Vassar, Grace's courses were very popular because of her teaching methods.

 Grace was the first woman in Yale's 233-year history to earn a doctorate in math.

She was always trying to think of new ways to make the material interesting and applicable. For example, she had students draw maps and create whole imaginary worlds while learning mechanical drawing.

Ask & Answer

What teaching methods do you find you learn the most from?

Disney cartoons were just starting to become popular, so it was natural that Grace would have her students develop drawings for animation. Because rocketry was a fascinating new subject at the time, Grace's students studied calculus, a type of math, by examining ballistics.

In this way, the material Grace's students learned in her classes was a part of the world they lived in. The topics did not exist only in textbooks.

Grace's life was very full with teaching and learning. Her husband, whom she called Hopper, also led a very busy life. They didn't see much of each other and they didn't have any children. Grace and her husband decided to separate and live in different houses in 1941. They later divorced in 1945.

WORLD WAR II

The United States entered World War II in 1941, after the Japanese attacked Pearl Harbor. The war in Europe between Germany and the other European countries had started in 1938. Many men joined the U.S. Army and Navy to support the fight against Germany and Japan. It was a time of patriotism, when people were willing to make sacrifices for their country.

Women were already allowed to serve in the Navy as nurses and in some administrative positions. Once the Navy Women's Reserve was established in 1942, however, many more women could join and there were more roles open to them.

 World War II was a time of patriotism, when people were willing to make sacrifices for their country.

At age 35, Grace was over the age limit. And at just 105 pounds, she was under the required weight. But she was determined to convince the U.S. Navy that it should accept her.

Pearl Harbor Video Games

Game developers often base games on history. One popular moment in history used in games is the attack on Pearl Harbor, which happened on December 7, 1941. Pearl Harbor was a naval base that was attacked by 353 Japanese fighter planes, bombers, and torpedo planes. The Japanese wanted to damage the U.S. Pacific Fleet so badly that the United States would not be able to join the war.

All eight of the U.S. battleships stationed there were damaged. Four of them sunk, while 2,403 Americans

were killed and 1,178 were injured. The United States declared war on Japan the next day.

Video games based on Pearl Harbor include flight simulators and online defense games. These can be played alone or with multiple players. Why are historical events such as Pearl Harbor so inspiring for video game designers?

Women in the Navy weren't treated the same as men in the 1940s. They were considered emergency personnel. It was only because many people in the government thought there wouldn't be enough men to fight the war that women were accepted. Women were signed on for only the duration of the war plus six months, and they could only serve on land in the United States.

Ask & Answer

How might technology be used to help prevent future attacks like Pearl Harbor on the United States?

There were also limitations on how far women could rise in rank. While the Navy had predicted about 10,000 women would sign up, by the end of the war almost 100,000 women had committed to serving.

Grace was finally granted entrance to the Navy in 1943. She excelled during her training and was made a lieutenant. She thought she might be sent to Washington, D.C., to work with one of her old teachers.

Instead, the Navy sent Grace to Harvard University in Boston, Massachusetts. There was a computer there that had recently been taken over by the Navy. Mathematicians were needed to work with it.

Computer scientists were just discovering what they could do with computers. Some people thought computers could only be used to figure out math problems. Other people felt sure computers would never be able to process information faster than humans could process it.

On the day Grace arrived at Harvard, she spent a few hours looking for the Bureau of Ships Computation Project. Finally, she found it in a basement. Her new boss, Howard H. Aiken, was a gruff, busy man who handed her a codebook. He said she had a week to learn how to program the large, loud machine called the Mark I.

  **The iPod or smartphone you might carry in your pocket is far more powerful than the computer Grace worked on at Harvard.**

Computers were much larger and less powerful than they are now. In fact, the iPod or smartphone you might carry in your pocket is far more powerful than the computer Grace worked on at Harvard.

The Navy had taken over Harvard's Mark I to use it to solve math problems. Some of those math problems had to do with new technology. This technology included using radar and protecting ships from magnetic mines. It was also used to discover the reach of the explosion produced by an atomic bomb, which is a large bomb that uses nuclear energy.

Bugs!

Have you ever heard of debugging a system? It's what people do to make sure any problems have been removed from their computers. While problems had long been referred to as "bugs," it was Grace who first used the word "debug." And that word arose from a real bug!

One day in 1947, a computer at Harvard called the Mark II wasn't working well. Grace discovered a moth that had shorted one of the connections in the machine. That dead moth was put into the pages of a notebook to mark the origin of a new term.

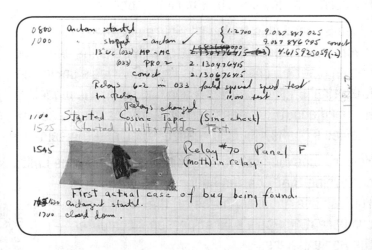

The Mark I looked very different from the computers you might have at home or at school today. It took up an entire room! This early computer was about 50 feet long (15 meters) and 8 feet tall (2.5 meters). It had more than 750,000 parts, used 530 miles (853 kilometers) of wire, and had 3,000,000 wire connections. It could add and subtract in three-tenths of a second and took a little more than 14 seconds to divide.

Howard H. Aiken & Charles Babbage

Remember reading about Charles Babbage and his Difference Machine in the introduction to this book? It turns out that Howard H. Aiken, Grace's supervisor at Harvard, was inspired by Charles Babbage.

When Howard was trying to figure out the kind of machine he needed to do fast calculations, he was shown a set of brass wheels from Charles's unfinished Analytical Engine. Charles's son had given the wheels to Harvard about 50 years earlier. After reading a set of Charles's books, Howard realized they had the same idea.

Howard was lucky that he got to see his machine built, something that Charles never was able to do. You can see several photos of the Mark I, and compare it to Apple's first personal computer, the Apple 1, here.

"Howard H. Aiken" Mark I vs Apple I 🔍

Today, you can simply type a math problem into a calculator or computer and it will give you an answer. But in the early days of computers, a user needed to translate the math problem into a language the computer understood. This was done using a codebook.

Have you ever seen an old-fashioned player piano reading a roll of music? Early computers used similar technology. A computer user punched the right code for a math problem into a roll of 4-inch-wide tape with a manual tape punch. Then the tape was fed through the computer to read in a very similar way that the player piano read the roll of music.

 When Grace first joined the team at Harvard, Howard didn't really want a woman working in the laboratory.

Howard H. Aiken and Grace got along well because they both saw themselves as part of a large, important group: the U.S. Navy. Howard was a demanding boss, but Grace thrived on hard work and responsibility.

Howard was a man who valued efficiency and hard work. He also valued people who worked hard! When Grace first joined the team at Harvard, Howard didn't really want a woman working in the laboratory. Remember, this was back when women weren't usually seen working outside the home. Many years later, when asked what Grace had been like to work with, Howard said, "Grace was a good man."

BETTER TO ASK FOR FORGIVENESS

Grace realized that computers had the potential to be faster and more useful than the Mark I. After she left Harvard, Grace went on to work at the Eckert-Mauchly Corp. as a senior mathematician. Her team was developing a brand new computer called the UNIVAC.

Later, the company was bought by the Sperry Corp. Grace stayed on, eventually becoming the systems engineer and director of automatic programming for the Universal Automatic Computer (UNIVAC) division. She worked for Sperry until 1971 and stayed connected with the company as it evolved into other companies.

The UNIVAC held information on high-speed magnetic tape instead of on tape with holes punched into it, which made it much faster. But programming mistakes were still common. Grace was eager to prevent those mistakes before they even happened.

Her solution was to invent a compiler. Grace's compiler could read shorter math codes and translate them into longer machine codes, which the computer could understand. This innovation saved a lot of time. It also resulted in programmers making far fewer mistakes since they were working with much shorter numbers. The compiler did the work of translating the numbers.

 Sometimes it's hard for people to recognize that there are new, better ways of doing things.

The people Grace worked for weren't impressed with her work on compilers. Companies are in business to make money, and by using Grace's compilers, the managers were taking a big risk. If the compilers didn't perform correctly, the company could lose money. Sometimes it's hard for people to recognize that there are new, better ways of doing things.

Cool Career: Web Developer

The Internet is a place to find knowledge, entertainment, and friends. Web developers are the people who make the Internet look and behave the way it does. They design web pages and figure out how to make the Internet experience efficient, friendly, and global, meaning that people from around the world can use it.

Grace pursued her ideas anyway. She kept improving her compilers and began working on developing computer languages. Her belief had always been, "It's better to ask for forgiveness than permission."

She suspected that machines could read letters as well as they could read numbers. After all, letters are symbols, just as numbers are symbols. It would be far easier for programmers to work with letter-based languages rather than use numbers for everything. Letters can be checked more easily by other people.

Grace and her team developed FLOW-MATIC, to be used on UNIVAC to do things such as figure out bills and payments for a company. Later, they used their work on FLOW-MATIC to help create a programming language called COBOL, which came out in 1959.

COBOL is a standard computer language for businesses. Because it uses regular English words, it's much easier for companies to use than programming languages that use numbers.

COBOL

COBOL is an acronym for "common business oriented language." COBOL is the second-oldest high-level programming language. It is mostly used for business, finance, and administrative purposes, such as payroll and billing for companies and governments.

Grace kept her ties with the Navy and with the academic world even as she worked for private companies. She served as a lecturer for different schools, including Harvard, the University of Pennsylvania, and George Washington University.

Her retirement from the Navy in 1966 came after reaching the rank of commander. Just one year later, she returned to the Navy. During the next 20 years, Grace rose to the rank of rear admiral. When she retired in 1986, at 80 years old, she was the oldest active duty officer in the United States.

Ask & Answer

What does innovation mean to you? Do you like to find better ways of doing things?

NOT A QUIET RETIREMENT

Even after her retirement, Grace worked as a senior consultant at Digital Equipment Corp. This was a company that produced computers and components. She served on many committees and spoke at lots of conferences, particularly ones on the importance of computer science education.

Grace Hopper received many awards during her career for her work in technology. She was the first woman to be elected Distinguished Fellow of the British Computer Society.

Grace Explains Nanoseconds

Grace even appeared on television on the *Late Show with David Letterman*! Here, and in front of many classrooms, Grace gave a quick explanation of a nanosecond. This is a billionth of a second. She showed a piece of wire that represents the maximum distance that light or electricity can travel in a nanosecond. The wire was nearly 12 inches long! She also used a prop to show the length of a picosecond. This is a thousandth of a nanosecond, or about the size of a tiny piece of pepper!

You can see a clip of her visit to a classroom here.

"Grace Hopper" explains nanoseconds 🔍

Grace was also the first woman to be awarded the National Medal of Technology. This important honor is given to American inventors and innovators who have made significant contributions to the development of new and important technology.

The Anita Borg Institute, a group that promotes women in technology, sponsors a conference called the Grace Hopper Celebration of Women in Computing.

 In 2013, Grace was even honored with a Google doodle on her birthday!

Many nicknames show how much people respected her. These include "Amazing Grace" and "Queen of Software." She is remembered as a pioneer, a person passionate about her field. In 2013, Grace was even honored with a Google doodle on her birthday! A woman who wasn't afraid to enter territory that was new to both men and women, she died in 1992 at the age of 85.

"The most important thing I've accomplished, other than building the compiler, is training young people. They come to me and say, 'Do you think we can do this?' I say, 'Try it.' And I back 'em up. They need that. I keep track of them as they get older and I stir 'em up at intervals so they don't forget to take chances."

—Grace Hopper

Chapter 3

SHAUNDRA BRYANT DAILY

We often think of technology as being based on logic and calculations. We think technology has no room for emotions, such as anger or joy. Computers only have emotions in science fiction books and movies! But people tend to be emotional more often than logical, and people are the ones who invent and use technology. Shaundra Bryant Daily believes technology and emotion are interconnected.

Born in 1979, Shaundra is now an electrical engineer teaching at Clemson University in South Carolina. She uses the connection between technology and emotions to teach students about programming.

Learning to code is an important skill, and Shaundra helps make it fun for kids. She works to develop programs that teach programming. Interactive experiences played out in a virtual world keep the learning fun.

CALLING DR. BRYANT

When Shaundra was growing up, her mother was a very positive influence. Joan Bryant used to call for Shaundra by pretending to page her over an intercom. "She'd say, 'Dr. Bryant, calling Dr. Bryant,' whenever she wanted to get my attention," Shaundra laughs. She even bought Shaundra a medical kit with a real stethoscope. This was Joan's way of telling Shaundra that she could be anything she wanted.

 When Shaundra was growing up, her mother, Joan, was a very positive influence.

Joan didn't have that same encouragement when she was growing up in New Orleans, Louisiana. Her own mother, who had worked as a maid all her life, explained to Joan that she could be a secretary or a maid.

Joan chose secretary, and that's what she did. But when she had a daughter, Joan wanted Shaundra to have a lot more choices.

Shaundra had encouragement from her dad and uncle, too. "They were very good at math and were always quizzing me. My interest in math probably came from that," she says.

What Shaundra really wanted to do was work for the F.B.I. After her high school chemistry teacher set up a crime scene for students to investigate, Shaundra realized that forensic science is just another way to solve puzzles, and she'd always loved puzzles.

Ask & Answer

Do you have encouraging adults in your life? Is this important? Why?

After graduating from high school, Shaundra went to Florida State University, where she had the option of choosing criminology or engineering as a major. Because she had always liked math and science, she chose engineering.

At first, Shaundra studied civil engineering, which involves the design of physical things, such as roads, buildings, and bridges. Soon, though, she realized that she found electrical engineering far more fascinating. She earned her bachelor's degree in electrical engineering from Florida State and her master's degree from Florida A&M University.

 Shaundra realized she liked electrical engineering more than civil engineering.

After that she traveled north to Boston to Massachusetts Institute of Technology, where she earned a master's of science and a PhD. While at MIT, she worked in the Affective Computing Group and Future of Learning Group at MIT's Media Laboratory. Public Broadcasting Station (PBS) did a series of short documentaries on scientists there. Shaundra was included.

Shaundra told them about her first day in the Media Lab. That's when someone asked her if she was there as a secretary.

"Why is computer science a good field for women? For one thing, that's where the jobs are, and for another, the pay is better than for many jobs, and finally, it's easier to combine career and family."

—Madeleine M. Kunin, American politician

Lives of Scientists—on Video!

PBS's *NOVA* produces a series of short videos on different scientists who are doing work that might be interesting to young people. The series is called *The Secret Life of Scientists and Engineers*. The documentaries profile scientists and engineers who also have engaging outside interests. In Shaundra's case, It was dancing. You can watch all the videos here.

PBS NOVA Secret Life Scientists Engineers 🔍

"There's nothing wrong with being a secretary," she says in the documentary. "My mother's a secretary. But I was here to be a graduate student and I was here to be a scientist."

AFFECTIVE COMPUTING

What do you feel like eating for dinner? Who do you want to invite to your birthday party? Where do you want to go on vacation? Every decision we make involves both logic and emotion. You might realize that chicken and broccoli are good, healthy things to have for dinner, but maybe what you really want is chocolate ice cream.

Many people consider computers to be purely based on logic. It's true that you need to talk to computers in logical ways to make them understand. But emotion can also be a part of the technology experience.

At the Media Lab at MIT where Shaundra worked, researchers were experimenting with something called affective computing. This means using computers to recognize, understand, and act out human emotions. Why is this useful?

 What use could humans have for computers that recognize emotions?

MARGARET HAMILTON

Computers are a necessary part of sending spacecraft to the moon! Without computers to perform complex calculations at high speeds, people might never have made it to outer space.

Margaret Hamilton was important to NASA's *Apollo 11* mission, which was the first mission to land astronauts on the moon. She earned a B.A. in mathematics at Earlham University. As the director and supervisor of software programming at MIT, which was then working on the *Apollo 11* space mission, she was responsible for helping to create the onboard guidance software.

It turns out that there are many ways computers can help people with emotion. People with autism, for example, can use technology to better understand the emotions of people around them. Autism is a disease that interrupts the way people display and understand emotion. This can be confusing and isolating for people who have autism.

Computers that are able to perceive emotion can also be helpful in improving people's health and habits. One of the projects that has come out of the Media Lab at MIT is a wearable stress sensor that senses physical signs of stress and notifies you.

(PS)

The spacecraft required this software to navigate and land on the moon. This was in the 1960s, when software design was just being invented. Much of what Margaret did was completely new and innovative! She is even credited with inventing the term "software engineer."

You can see a picture of her with a stack of code she wrote for *Apollo 11*.

Another Media Lab project is a device that measures children's responses to playing games. Understanding how children react can help game developers design educational games and toys that kids like more.

> **Shaundra wondered how technology could connect people to their own emotions and to the emotions of others.**

Shaundra was interested in affective computing partly because she didn't think of herself as a very emotional person. When her parents threw her a surprise party, she was happy about it, but didn't get excited as most people would have. She simply told her parents, "Thank you." Shaundra wondered how technology could be used to better connect people to their own emotions and to the emotions of others.

G.I.R.L.S.

What do you and your friends do when you get together for a sleepover? Compare playlists on iPods, play video games, and talk?

Listening to a group of girls chat about their lives, Shaundra realized that they were processing their emotions. And they were getting feedback from their friends about how they felt and why.

How do you recognize your own emotions? Do you find your emotions useful? Are they ever confusing?

Shaundra wondered if a computer program could provide the same thing. Could it help girls process their emotions and give them feedback on why they felt the way they did about things?

Shaundra created the G.I.R.L.S. program while she was working in the Affective Computing Group at MIT. The acronym *G.I.R.L.S.* stands for Girls Involved In Real Life Sharing. It's a program that lets users create their own graphic novel–type stories about things that have happened in their lives.

Cool Career: IT Manager

People who use computers for work or fun often need help. Sometimes, computers feel very mysterious! That's when you call an IT, or information technology, manager for help. Many large companies have IT people on staff to maintain computers for the employees. Smaller organizations might hire freelance IT people to help only when they need it.

The program asks users to create different characters and captions for each picture. Users are also asked to think about the emotions portrayed in each picture.

The computer tries to decide what emotions the characters are feeling. The point of the program is to get kids thinking about their own emotions. Then they can reflect on how they might react differently in a similar situation in the future.

"My hope is that someday counselors will be able to use the program to work with kids in schools to talk about things going on in their lives or to reflect on things," says Shaundra.

PROFESSOR ROSALIND PICARD

Shaundra considers her advisor at MIT to have been a major influence in her work. Professor Rosalind Picard has several degrees in electrical engineering and computer science.

Before joining the faculty at the MIT Media Lab, Professor Picard worked for a company studying affective computing. Her work focused on integrating computers with emotions in a way that was healthy and useful.

TEACHING AND VENVI

After getting her PhD from MIT, Shaundra got a job as an assistant professor in the School of Computing at Clemson University in South Carolina.

She teaches classes with titles such as "Educational Technology" and "Human-Centered Computing Fundamentals." Do these sound intimidating? What Shaundra is really doing is teaching her students to think about ways of combining technology with education.

 Shaundra tries to come up with ways of teaching technology that are fun and useful.

Today, her inventions help people with autism, epilepsy, depression, dementia, and human-computer interactions. She says, "I want to invent the thing that enables us all to have better experiences in life."

Shaundra says of her advisor, "She took something she was passionate about that nobody else was looking at and made a real impact in that area, a unique contribution to the field." Shaundra admires Rosalind for her work in affective computing, and also for being a great mom to her three sons.

Do you do Hour of Code in your classroom? Do you ever play with Lego robotics? These are the kinds of subjects Shaundra discusses in her classes. She and her students try to come up with ways of teaching technology that are fun and useful.

A new program Shaundra has come up with at Clemson is called VENVI. This combines technology with movement. She wants to create an environment where learning is natural, exciting, and fun.

An important part of this work is called embodied ways of understanding. This is when people transfer the learning that their brains are doing into their own bodies. This helps them understand it.

PS

Try It Yourself!

You can explore VENVI's website here and even download programs that VENVI has offered before. Always ask an adult's permission before downloading anything onto a computer.

VENVI programs 🔍

Since about the age of 14, Shaundra has been a dancer. She has danced as part of competitive teams, at the schools she attended, and now in her kitchen with her daughters!

Dancing is as much a part of her life as technology. Working with embodied ways of understanding has allowed her to find a way to combine her passion for dancing with her passion for technology education. She and her team at Clemson University have created a virtual world in VENVI where students in grades 4 to 7 program their own characters to dance.

> **Shaundra has danced as part of competitive teams, at the schools she attended, and now in her kitchen with her daughters!**

"We started working with this in 2008 and really moved forward with it in 2012," Shaundra says. "The general idea is that we can reinforce understanding about different concepts by moving with our bodies. We have motion-capture suits that grab actions and cut them into little chunks, and a 3-D environment for students to work in." Sound like fun?

Shaundra explains that the students work on making their characters dance. "We replicate what we did using programming language and working with loops and sequences, stuff like that. It looks a lot like Scratch, but instead of making a game, you can make a character dance."

Not only does this program teach kids the programming skills they'll need when they start looking for jobs, it teaches them to think in logical ways about processes. This is important for any area, not only science and technology fields.

"We need to continue to expand opportunities for all students to become more interested in STEM fields. This is just another pathway to that," Shaundra says. And, of course, it's fun! How often is learning new dance moves part of school?

 VENVI teaches kids to think in logical ways about processes.

Get Moving, Get Learning

The more researchers learn about the brain, the more they understand that the brain and the body are very connected when it comes to learning.

When you're studying for a test, do you sit at a desk or stand on your head? Most of us sit at our desks. But some research shows we might learn better if we were doing something physical while we studied, or even before we studied. Movement makes our hearts pump faster and blood flow increase. This gets your brain's synapses firing and makes for great learning conditions. If you run around or spend some time dancing before you take a test, you're likely to get a better grade!

Shaundra performs alongside her virtual character.

"I love the flexibility and that I get to explore ideas that I'm interested in," says Shaundra. "This is the best job ever!"

MIXING KIDS WITH TECHNOLOGY

You might be surprised to discover that Shaundra, who spends several hours a day working on a computer, has strict limits on screen time for her kids! How many hours a week are you allowed to use a laptop or iPad or watch TV? For Shaundra's daughters, the limit is two hours a week.

"There's disagreement on the impact of kids being in front of screens for long periods of time," she says.

Do you have a lot or a little access to technology? Do you think this is helpful or not? Why?

"Some researchers think it can negatively impact brains. That's just enough of the unknown for me. We don't know yet how it affects people's brains when they sit in front of a screen for long times."

She laughs when she describes what her kids are like in front of the TV. "They watch it so rarely that they turn into zombies!" The Daily family has one iPad for the whole family. The kids are allowed to do only educational activities with the iPad.

Shaundra's children get plenty of benefit from having a techy mom, though. They've worked in Scratch, the programming interface for kids built by MIT. Plus they've made and edited videos. Perhaps the biggest benefit is having a mom who encourages creative thinking about systems, logic, and processes.

 Shaundra's children get plenty of benefit from having a techy mom.

"I want them to be introduced to it, because technology is ubiquitous, it's all around us, but I feel they can get enough of an introduction without overdoing it."

Another way they might get introduced to technology is from underneath Shaundra's desk at work! "From 3 p.m. to whenever they go to bed, around 7 p.m., that's their time," she says of her kids. Sometimes that means they come to Shaundra's office or to work-related events with her.

"My students know it and my colleagues know it. I used to have a boss who'd come in and look under my desk in the afternoons because he knew my kids like to hide under there and play!"

Babies at Work

Yahoo CEO Marissa Mayer had a unique solution to the question of what to do with her baby while she was at work. She had a nursery built right next door to her office!

This actually angered some of the employees who worked at Yahoo. Marissa had announced, soon after having her baby, that employees would no longer be allowed to work from home or telecommute. Many parents find telecommuting to be a very useful way to work while still being available for their kids. Marissa, however, felt that employees would be more productive if they were working in an office. What do you think?

PEOPLE IN TECHNOLOGY

Look around your classroom, or a restaurant, or a movie theater. There are lots of different kinds of people, right? Boys, girls, white people, African Americans, Asians, Latinos . . . and those are only the differences we can see. Everyone is very different on the inside, too. People are different in terms of how they think, how they move and talk, and what they're interested in.

 Look around your classroom. There are lots of different kinds of people.

When Shaundra was growing up, she knew people were different on the inside but she didn't always see them as different on the outside. "My mom never told me about race issues or gender issues," she says. "Part of it was we lived in predominantly white places when I was growing up, and people there weren't discussing racism or inequality issues. It just wasn't a conversation anyone was having."

Ask & Answer

Do people talk about race or gender at your school or in your home? What do you learn from these conversations?

Now, because of television and the Internet, there is a lot more access to stories about racism and sexism. When Shaundra was growing up, there weren't as many opportunities to discuss these things. And Shaundra's mom didn't think Shaundra needed to know about them.

"I never thought to myself, 'Oh, I'm a girl or I'm a minority, that means such and such.' I have never sat down in a class and felt uncomfortable, like I wasn't supposed to be there. I was smart enough to be there, and that was enough. I didn't even know being a girl or being black were ever obstacles! I was never afraid to go after anything because of how I looked."

 "I never thought to myself, 'Oh, I'm a girl or I'm a minority, that means such and such.'"

When Shaundra got to college, someone asked her if she was going to join the National Society of Black Engineers. "I didn't understand why black engineers needed their own organization," she laughs. She did end up becoming involved in the organization through friends.

Shaundra also learned more about how inequality can affect the careers of engineers. But Shaundra still feels that it's best to learn later in life that your looks can change your path. The worst thing would be to limit what you think you can do because of what you look like.

Shaundra is taking the same approach with her daughters that her mother took with her. Of course, the Internet exists and topics such as racism and sexism are talked about much more frequently. It's harder and harder to keep her children innocent of these topics.

"About a year and a half ago, they started discussing race in school and my daughters came home talking about it," Shaundra says. "My youngest pointed out that people have different color skin and I asked her what that meant. She said, 'I don't know!'"

Try It Yourself!

There are lots of opportunities to try your hand at programming, designing robots, and using technology in other wonderful ways! Check out the USA Science & Engineering Festival, where there are lots of exhibits geared toward kids interested in what technology can do! You can find more information at this website.

USA Science & Engineering Festival ○

"So I gave her this scientific explanation of the amount of melanin in different types of skin and she was satisfied. I know that eventually they'll be more exposed to those types of things, but I'm hard-pressed to introduce them at home as things they need to be worried about," she explains.

"When it comes time for them to go to summer camps, I don't know if I'll send them to girls' technology camps. If they're interested, I'll send them to tech camp, but maybe not a girls-only one. Are there special boys' tech camps? Why does there need to be a special girls' camp?"

Shaundra does believe that people need to see role models in different fields, so she participates in panels and discussions about women working in technology. "I do put myself out there and say, 'Hey, we're women, we exist in technology,' and I do that because I think it's important to see role models of everyone in every field."

 People need to see role models in different fields.

However, she presents being a woman in technology as something normal, not an obstacle women need to overcome. "It feels as though if you lead with obstacles and make them specific to women, it's as if we don't belong there in first place and need to prepare ourselves."

 Your gender has nothing to do with how smart you are and how hard you work.

As Shaundra points out, that's not true. Your gender has nothing to do with how smart you are and how hard you work. And it shouldn't determine what you can do.

In Her Own Words

You can hear Shaundra talk about her work in her own words here. Does she say anything that inspires you?

"Shaundra Daily" LiveScience machines 🔍

In the past, it has been difficult to find female and male role models in certain jobs. For example, men make up only about 2 percent of all preschool and kindergarten teachers in the United States.

Cool Career: Computer Programmer

Computer programmers are the people who translate human language into something computers can understand. They create a bridge between an engineer's vision and a user's reality. Everything you do with your smartphone, iPod, or computer was made possible by a computer programmer.

For a young man who wants to be a preschool teacher, it can be hard to find a man who works in that field to look up to. The same goes for girls who want to work in technology.

People such as Bill Gates, Mark Zuckerberg, and the late Steve Jobs are all common household names. Most people know who these men are. Do you know who Carol Bartz is? She's the former CEO of Yahoo. How about Ginni Rometty? She's the president and CEO of IBM. These are very powerful women in the field of computing.

Just as it's important for men to be working in jobs that are traditionally held by women, it's important for women to work in jobs traditionally held by men.

> Do you know who Carol Bartz is? She's the former CEO of Yahoo. How about Ginni Rometty? She's the president and CEO of IBM.

A Self-Fulfilling Prophecy

Have you ever heard of a self-fulfilling prophecy? A self-fulfilling prophecy is something that is not true, but because people believe it to be so, it becomes true.

During a science experiment in 1968, researchers gave elementary students a test. Then they told the teachers that some of the kids scored as unusually smart when they were actually average.

When the researchers gave the kids another test at the end of the year, who did well? The students they'd said were extra smart scored much better than the other students in the classroom. Because the teachers believed those students to be special, they'd treated them differently. They actually taught them better, so the children did better on the test. That's called a self-fulfilling prophecy.

Some scientists believe that if we tell people about discrimination, they might be more likely to experience it. What do you think?

SELF-FULFILLING PROPHECY

OUR ACTIONS

influence

impact

OUR BELIEFS

OTHERS BELIEFS

cause

reinforce

OTHER ACTIONS

Can you think of any self-fulfilling prophecies you might be affected by? What can you do to change them?

THE FUTURE IS BRIGHT!

Shaundra would like to continue her work at the intersection of emotions, movement, and technology.

"I would like to see technology heading in the direction where it's helping to heal relationships," she says. "All kinds of relationships—with yourself, online, parents and children, groups of people. There's a real opportunity to change how things are."

Shaundra's commitment to the idea of relationships is evident when she talks about what her perfect day would look like. "I would go bowling, go to the movies, hit up a car show, and end it with dancing," she laughs. Hmmm . . . nowhere does she mention working on her computer as part of a perfect day!

When asked if she has any advice for girls interested in technology, she gives an answer that is inspiring far beyond any particular person or field: "Where your passion meets the world's needs, that's your calling."

Chapter 4

JEAN YANG

Jean Yang didn't always know she was going to be a computer scientist. But if you look at her upbringing, it provides a few clues! She had two parents who were involved in the technology field. Even though she went to a school with a strong humanities program, she decided to pursue computer science as a career. She earned her bachelor's degree in computer science from Harvard and she's finishing her PhD at Massachusetts Institute of Technology.

Jean works primarily with programming languages, which she describes as "incredibly powerful." She's interested in how people communicate with machines and she's fascinated by the problems that can arise.

SEEDS OF SCIENCE

Until she was about five years old, Jean lived with her grandparents in China. She didn't have a tablet or an iPod—in fact, there were very few technological gadgets in the house.

"Even paper was expensive, so I had a little chalkboard to draw on," says Jean, who was born in 1987. "I did a lot of arts and a fair amount of crafts!"

Perhaps it was this early need to be imaginative in her play that led her to pursue a career in computer science. You may not think this is true, but computer science is a very creative profession.

Ask & Answer

Do you think having lots of toys makes kids more or less creative?

Maybe Jean developed an early fascination with technology because there was so little of it in her early childhood house. Or maybe her desire to code started when she moved with her mother to the United States to join her father, who was finishing his PhD in computer science.

 You may not think this is true, but computer science is a very creative profession.

This was when computers became a major part of Jean's life. Her dad's office at Carnegie Mellon University was home to several computers and Jean spent a lot of time there. Her family got their first personal computer in 1994.

Jean was allowed to play games on this computer. "Most of the games were designed to improve my cognitive ability or my knowledge of academic trivia," Jean says. "*Brain Quest* was one of my parents' favorites."

Game On!

Do you play educational computer games? Video games have been used for decades to help kids learn math, reading, science, and lots of other topics.

Starting in the 1990s, educational games became more popular as more people owned home computers. Parents and teachers realized they could combine learning with fun on the screen. Do you think you learn better with video games or with books? Does it depend on the subject?

You can try free online games at these sites, or find your own!

free educational computer games brainPOP 🔍

Many kids are lucky enough to have parents who let them play computer games, especially now. But Jean's parents went a step further and taught her how to code.

"My parents used Visual Basic and taught me how to use it when I was in elementary school." Often, an early experience with a skill, such as programming, means a person will have an easier time learning the more advanced version of the skill later on.

 Jean's parents taught her how to code. She also learned programming in elementary school.

Jean also learned programming in elementary school. "Our homeroom teacher used to take us with our floppy discs to the basement computer room and we would make little Logo pictures!"

Floppy discs were what people used to store data on in the early days of personal computers. This was before the Internet and before USB drives.

Floppy disc from 1984

Visualize Visual Basic

Visual Basic was created by Microsoft in 1991. It was one of the first to use a drag-and-drop design. Users are able to choose the controls they want to introduce, such as text boxes or buttons, and drag them to what's called the form, which is the field on which programming takes place. Then they can reprogram the values of the controls so they look just how the user wants them to look.

Visual Basic is considered a good programming language to learn if you are a beginner. Search online and you'll find many tutorials.

Women at Carnegie Mellon

Jean's father worked at Carnegie Mellon University, which has become known as a school that does an excellent job attracting women who want to study computer science. At most universities, men far outnumber female graduates in computer science programs. At Carnegie Mellon, however, women make up 40 percent of computer science graduates.

Part of the reason is that the university offers formal mentoring programs. Because there have always been more men in computer science courses, they already have a network of other men to look up to and get advice from. Carnegie Mellon offers women that same type of support, plus tutoring, in a more structured way. Women get to meet role models who have already done this type of work and succeeded, which can be very empowering. Do you have role models you look up to?

Now, many schools are able to offer every student a computer to use. But when computers were first starting to become fixtures in schools, there were far fewer computers than there were students.

Basement computer labs such as the one at Jean's school weren't unusual. Computers were much more expensive then, and they weren't anywhere near as powerful as they are now.

> **The entire roomful of computers that helped guide the first spacecraft onto the surface of the moon in 1966 had less processing ability than a calculator today!**

There were no laptops or tablets. There were just bulky desktops for kids to share while they learned the basics of computer programming. In fact, the entire roomful of computers that helped guide the first spacecraft onto the surface of the moon in 1966 had less processing ability than a calculator today!

Jean attended an all-girls school for middle school and high school. While the school was known for its excellent humanities programs, which includes the arts and languages, it also offered lots of classes in sciences, math, and programming.

Jean found that she excelled in her English classes. She loved literature and writing and used her time in high school to develop her writing voice. In addition to her regular school classes, Jean took extra classes and summer programs at Carnegie Mellon University. She learned statistics and programming, and even worked with robots.

Ask & Answer

Is computer programming more of a group activity or one you do by yourself? Why?

Try It Yourself!

Are you interested in learning to code? Play around with the cute monster at this website. What do you learn from playing with the code on this page? Is playing a game a good way to learn something?

Crunchzilla code monster 🔍

When she decided that she would study either engineering or computer science in college, some of her teachers thought differently. They told her they thought she'd return to the humanities before too long. "Maybe they thought that the humanities were a more worthwhile pursuit than something that seemed more like a trade skill," says Jean.

Some teachers told Jean they thought she'd return to the humanities before too long.

A trade skill is a learned skill that you perform for an income. Cooking, plumbing, carpentry, and sewing are all trade skills. Sometimes, people consider jobs in the trade industry to be less desirable than academic jobs in areas such as science, math, or literature.

And sometimes, people think it's the opposite, that academic jobs are less desirable than trade jobs!

Jean wonders if this is one reason why her teachers didn't take her seriously when she said she was going to go into computer science. "Engineering and computer science seem to have a bad reputation as being 'useful' rather than 'intellectual.'"

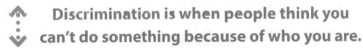

Discrimination is when people think you can't do something because of who you are.

Jean also discovered resistance to her career choice in the form of discrimination. That's when someone thinks you can't do something because you're a girl, or because you're a boy, or because you're an African American or because you are left-handed.

In Jean's case, the discrimination was more careless than mean. Friends of her parents said things like, "You're too pretty to study computer science," and that MIT "wasn't a place for girls." Despite these comments from other people, Jean knew she was making the right choice for herself.

Ask & Answer

What does it feel like to be discriminated against? What can you do about it?

Cool Career: Nanotechnology

We've seen computers shrink since they were first invented and they're still getting smaller! Nanotechnology is technology at a very tiny size. For example, scientists are trying to design robots small enough to fit into blood vessels. These robots can be used to perform surgery inside a patient's body without having to cut it open.

IMPOSTOR SYNDROME

When she got to Harvard, Jean had more hurdles to leap over. She liked her classes, but felt as if she didn't belong. "I didn't have much confidence in myself," she says. "I figured that everyone except me was qualified to be there. There's a term for this— impostor syndrome."

Impostor syndrome is a psychological condition. It can happen when you have trouble seeing your own success.

Maybe you keep getting A's on your math tests, but you still feel as if you are bad at math. Maybe you score plenty of points during your basketball games, but still feel like you aren't a good player. This might be an example of impostor syndrome.

Jean found that she wasn't comfortable answering questions in her classes, where there were only a few women. "I remember my advisor asking me why I wasn't speaking up in class. I told her that I felt like everyone else had better things to say. She pointed out that the guys who were talking only had good things to say about half the time—the key was to speak up."

This realization helped Jean gain some confidence. She started to understand that she would probably say good things in class at least as often as her classmates.

Another thing that helped was when a classmate discovered the class's midterm grades in an unprotected document on the department server. Jean had the second-highest score! "I figured the midterm had just been really easy," she says. Her score was another clue that she was heading in the direction that was right for her.

Ask & Answer

Have you ever been surprised by your own performance, either in class or in a club or when doing something at home? How did that make you feel?

INFLUENCES

Ask any professional and she'll tell you she had lots of help getting to where she is. A strong, positive influence is almost always essential for a successful career.

Jean had many role models. Several of her high school teachers made her think deeply about learning and about the world and her place in it. The ability to think critically and creatively about yourself is a great tool to have, no matter what you decide to study later on.

Try It Yourself

Have you ever been to a maker faire? A maker faire can be a good chance to try your hand at creating robots, video games, gadgets, and more! They are gatherings of people who are interested in arts, crafts, science projects, and making stuff themselves. Lots of people who are interested in technology attend maker faires. They take place around the country, including the White House, and are popping up in other countries, including Egypt!

Visit these sites for information on maker faires.

maker faire information makezine

Ask any professional and she'll tell you she had lots of help getting to where she is.

Jean found more influences in college. Even though she thought about changing her major many times during college, her advisor, Margo Seltzer, helped her remain focused on her goals.

She was the one who noticed Jean wasn't speaking up in class and asked why. She also taught Jean about impostor syndrome. Often, if you can recognize and label a problem, it becomes much easier to handle. It also helps to know you're not alone in feeling doubtful or anxious or uncertain.

Jean says of Margo, "Every time she felt like self-doubt was getting in my way, she talked me out of it and pushed me forward. If it hadn't been for her, I don't know that I would have stuck with it."

"The world would be a better place if more engineers, like me, hated technology. The stuff I design, if I'm successful, nobody will ever notice. Things will just work and be self-managing."

—Radia Perlman, inventor of several programming languages

Other professors and advisors helped Jean by making suggestions about the courses she should take. They showed her what it means to do research. They guided her in what it means to be in the academic world instead of working for a corporation.

These role models showed her how to approach decisions about her life and work. One role model, Greg Morrisett, even inspired her to pursue the work she's doing now researching programming languages.

Another role model was a female professor named Radhika Nagpal. She was a new professor who was just starting during Jean's freshman year.

MARGO SELTZER

When giving a talk about her work as a woman in technology, Margo Seltzer, Jean's advisor at Harvard, starts by showing pictures. She shows pictures of her kids, her cats, her husband, cakes she's made, and friends she met while following a women's soccer team around Germany. Her life beyond the computer lab is very full! Luckily, she has a lot of energy.

She earned a degree from Harvard and worked for a few different startup companies, then went to graduate school at the University of California, Berkeley, before returning to Harvard as a professor.

TECHNOLOGY

These role models supported Jean right when she needed it most. They showed her how to approach decisions about both her life and her work.

Jean also gets lots of inspiration from professionals in a completely different field. Is it surprising that this field is music?

"There are various similarities between academia and the music industry. Part of it is about talent, but a lot of it is luck and how your work is perceived by a more general audience," says Jean.

PS

he has a few words of advice for women. The rst is what she learned from growing up with wo older brothers: "Be the smart girl." The second piece of dvice came from the years she spent working for startup ompanies: "Take risks, learn stuff, do things you love."

he third came from her years spent as a professor: "You hould always have three things in your life you care assionately about. Maybe one of them is work, one of nem is people, and there should be something else. If ny one of them isn't going well, you'll still ave two sources of strength." You can watch er video talk here.

"Margo Seltzer" inspiring women in technology 🔍

Jean finds it inspiring to see female musical artists succeeding in a male-dominated field. A couple of her favorites are Nicki Minaj and St. Vincent. "Being successful involves not only doing good work but also having a strong brand, as well as swagger!"

Jean not only appreciates the role models she had growing up, she also wants the opportunity to be a role model to girls who are just entering the field. "I give talks to middle and high school girls and write online for younger women interested in STEM. I'd like to be one of the women young girls point to and say, 'That can be me when I grow up.'"

Jean's Role Models

Jean takes a lot of inspiration from her role models. She even wrote up a list and posted it on Quora, which is a question-and-answer website where people write and edit questions and answers on a range of topics. One of her role models is Grace Hopper! You can read Jean's list of influential role models here.

 "Jean Yang," superstar role models 🔍

Grace Hopper

Like Daughter Like Mom

Jean's mom is a computer scientist as well! She was a professor of computer science when the family lived in China, and got her master's degrees in biostatistics and information sciences when they moved to the United States. She worked as a biostatistician for several years and has been working as a software engineer for more than a decade.

FOR THE LOVE OF THE JOB

When Jean first decided to pursue computer science, people used to tell her she'd be sitting in a room coding all day long. "You're going to be lonely," she was warned. But the reality is very different.

"I work with brilliant, interesting people" Jean says. "I like how the people in my field think—they are very logical and often have great senses of humor."

Cool Career: Computer Game Developer

Do you like playing computer games? How about designing your own? Game developers come up with ideas for new games and decide how those games are going to work. Then they program and test the games before other people get to try them. Sound like fun?

Jean loves the international aspect of her job in research. Because computer science is a global industry, she works with people around the world. She travels to different countries for conferences and collaboration. "I have friends all over the world."

Jean finds the work itself fascinating. Coding is a very logical process, but it also requires creative thinking. "I get to think about what the world might look like in 5, 10, 20 years from now," she says.

"A ship in port is safe, but that is not what ships are for. Sail out to sea and do new things."

—Grace Hopper, American computer scientist

"I get to imagine a world in which computers are faster and people are more reasonable. I get to think about how people will be expressing their ideas in the future." When you write a computer program, you need to think about how machines process language. But you also need to think about how the users—people—process language.

 Coding is a very logical process, but it also requires creative thinking.

"Like spoken languages, programming languages allow people to capture and communicate some unit of meaning," Jean says. "Unlike spoken languages, we have the power to design programming languages to suit our needs."

Spoken languages evolve naturally within societies through many hundreds of years. Computer languages are different because they are built during a much shorter period of time. Imagine what spoken language would sound like if humans had invented it only 5 or 10 years ago.

Ask & Answer

Why is it healthy to have a job that you love to do? What would your life be like if you dreaded going to work every day?

The Turing Award

Jean cites Fran Allen as one of her role models. She is an American computer scientist who was the first women to win the Turing Award in 2006. A Turing Award is granted to leaders in the computer field and is considered to be the same level of honor as the Nobel Prize.

The award is named after Alan Turing, a British mathematician who invented the Turing machine. This wasn't an actual machine, but a way of thinking logically that helped codebreakers during World War II. He worked with many other people at a place called Bletchley Park, trying to break the code that the Germans were using for communication. About 75 percent of the people working at Bletchley Park were women.

In early 2015, during a renovation project at Bletchley Park, builders discovered some of Turing's notes stuffed into the roof as insulation. You can view the notes. What do you do with your notes from school or your own projects? Do you think people will read them 50 years from now?

"Alan Turing" notes in Bletchley Park 🔍

> **Jean's research lies in designing new programming languages to make it easier for programmers to write programs.**

"One thing I spend my time doing is thinking about how to design language constructs that help people write the programs they intended to write," explains Jean. "In spoken languages, this would be equivalent to coming up with a new word or a new sentence structure. I spend a lot of time thinking about the kinds of programs that people have trouble writing and what might make it easier."

Jean's research lies in designing new programming languages. To do this, she has to think about how people interact with the world today and how they might interact in the future. She has to have a terrific imagination to think about things that don't even exist yet!

Jean hopes to find a position as a professor at a top research university. As she says, though, "getting there involves some amount of luck!"

"I believe that technology should give us superpowers."

—Hilary Mason, data scientist, founder of Fast Forward Labs

Jean loves her research, but there's more to life than working. "I love writing and crafting. I would love to get into writing creative nonfiction or even fiction, but most of the time I write about what it's like to be a graduate student, what it's like to study computer science, and what it's like to be a woman in a field mostly filled by men.

"It's important to me that people understand my world. So I spend a lot of time thinking about how to explain all the different parts of it—my actual work and also the environment I work in."

 Jean loves her research, but there's more to life than working.

ADVICE TO FUTURE COOL WOMEN

Jean thinks it's important to talk to young women about what it's like to be a woman in a job where there are mostly men. She gives talks to middle- and high school-aged girls and writes articles about her own experiences and what she's learned.

"Most of us don't go a day—an hour, even— without using complex software on our phones and laptops," she says. "Technology is starting to run our lives. Being interested in technology means being interested in how everyone's life is going to look."

Why is it important to try to inspire other people?

Jean has this advice for girls who are interested in technology: "To the girls who want to go for it, don't be afraid to go hard." Jean understands, better than most people, that going for it will involve getting out of your comfort zone. It means doing and saying things that feel surprising.

"There will be hard parts. People might tell you that you can't do it. People might not always pick you first for their team. People might make you feel like it's weird to try so hard because girls are supposed to be 'sweet' or 'gentle.' Stay focused on what you want to do. It will get better—and keep being better."

She also believes that role models can make a huge difference, just as they did for her. "Find people in your life who inspire you and support you," she suggests. "If someone does both, hold on to them! Find people you can look up to as role models. Find people who think you are awesome and who want to help you and let them support you."

And then, maybe most importantly, she turns that around and says, "Don't forget to be kind and to inspire and support other people whenever you can."

TIMELINE

1824

- Ada Lovelace works with Charles Babbage on the Analytical Machine. She is often described as the first computer programmer because she developed the very first algorithm meant to be processed by a machine.

1940s

- An Austrian American actress named Hedy Lamarr, widely known as one of the most beautiful women in Hollywood, co-invents a new technology used in guiding torpedoes during WW II. It is eventually incorporated into today's wireless technology.

1942

- Women work as WREN (Women's Royal Navy Service) Colossus operators during World War II in Bletchley Park, England. Colossus was the world's first electronic, digital, programmable computer, and was used by British codebreakers to help read encrypted German messages.

- ENIAC (Electronic Numerical Integrator And Computer) is developed during World War II, funded by the U.S. government. The machine is programmed by six women: Kay McNulty, Betty Jennings, Betty Snyder, Marlyn Wescoff, Fran Bilas, and Ruth Lichterman.

1952

- Grace Hopper develops the first compiler for an electronic computer. She goes on to help develop the computer language COBOL.

1965

- Mary Allen Wilkes becomes the first person to use a computer in a private home.

- Sister Mary Kenneth Keller becomes the first American woman to earn a PhD in computer science. Her thesis is titled "Inductive Inference on Computer Generated Patterns."

1972

- Karen Spärck Jones introduces the concept of inverse document frequency weighting, used in information retrieval. It provides the foundation for many of today's search engines.

1974

- Jean E. Sammet becomes the first female president of the Association for Computing Machinery.

1978

- The Association for Women in Computing is founded in Washington, D.C.

TIMELINE

1979

- Carol Shaw becomes the first woman to program and design a video game, which is called *3-D Tic-Tac-Toe* and is played on the Atari 2600.

1980s

- Shafi Goldwasser works with Silvio Micali on zero-knowledge proofs, which provide the foundation of cryptography. Today's Internet security is built on this foundation.

1984

- Roberta Williams does pioneering work in graphical adventure games for personal computers, particularly the *King's Quest* series, which is first released in 1984.

1985

- Radia Perlman invents the spanning-tree protocol, which is essential to today's Internet.

1989

- Frances E. Allen becomes the first female IBM Fellow. Later, in 2006, Allen is the first female recipient of the Association for Computing Machinery's Turing Award. The award is named after Alan Turing, a British mathematician who worked during World War II to break German code.

1993

- Barbara Liskov and Jeannette Wing develop the Liskov substitution principle, which contributes to the development of programming languages.

1997

- Anita Borg becomes the founding director of the Institute for Women and Technology.

1999

- Marissa Mayer becomes the first female engineer hired at Google. She becomes the CEO of Yahoo in 2012.

2005

- Ruchi Sanghvi becomes the first female engineer at Facebook.

2009

- Manuela Veloso receives the ACM/SIGART Autonomous Agents Research Award for her work in artificial intelligence.

2012

- Sheryl Sandberg becomes the first female member of Facebook's board of directors.

2014

- For the first time, more women than men enroll in a University of California, Berkeley, introductory computer class.

ASK & ANSWER

Introduction

- How does technology affect your life? What would your life be like without technology?

Chapter 1

- Computers used to be huge and now they can be very small. What effect does the size of computers have on their availability? Why?

- What will the computer industry be like 20 years from now if one gender continues to work in it the most?

Chapter 2

- Do you have any skills or interests that you might turn into a career?

- Have you ever been in a dangerous situation that you saved yourself from? What did you learn from the experience?

- How does society's opinions affect you? If society thought you should only have a certain type of job, would you follow that suggestion?

- What teaching methods do you find you learn the most from?

- How might technology be used to help prevent future attacks like Pearl Harbor on the United States?

- What does innovation mean to you? Do you like to find better ways of doing things?

Chapter 3

- Do you have encouraging adults in your life? Is this important? Why?

- How do you recognize your own emotions? Do you find your emotions useful? Are they ever confusing?

- Does anyone inspire you like Rosalind inspires Shaundra? Why is it important to have mentors?

- Do you have a lot or a little access to technology? Do you think this is helpful or not? Why?

- Do people talk about race or gender at your school or in your home? What do you learn from these conversations?

- Can you think of any self-fulfilling prophecies you might be affected by? What can you do to change them?

Chapter 4

- Do you think having lots of toys makes kids more or less creative?

- Is computer programming more of a group activity or one you do by yourself? Why?

- What does it feel like to be discriminated against? What can you do about it?

- Have you ever been surprised by your own performance, either in class or in a club or when doing something at home? How did that make you feel?

- Why is it healthy to have a job that you love to do? What would your life be like if you dreaded going to work every day?

- Why is it important to try to inspire other people?

academic: relating to education.

affective computing: using computers to recognize, understand, and act out human emotions.

algorithm: a set of steps that are followed to solve a mathematical problem or to complete a computer process.

amputate: to cut off.

anomaly: something that is not what you would expect.

app: a program that runs on a phone, tablet, or other computerized device.

artificial: manmade.

ballistics: the science that studies the movement of objects that are shot through the air.

biology: the study of life and of living things.

biostatistics: statistics, or numbers, that show facts about biology.

civilization: a community of people that is advanced in art, science, and government.

code: another name for a computer program or the act of writing a computer program.

cognitive: activities related to thinking, understanding, learning, and remembering.

collaborate: to work with others.

communicate: to share information in some way.

compiler: a computer program that translates language into a language a computer can understand.

computer: a device for storing and working with information.

computer science: the study of computers and how they work.

constructs: parts of something.

consultant: a person who provides expert advice.

convention: the way things are usually done.

convey: to make an idea understandable.

criminology: the scientific study of crime and criminals.

dementia: a brain condition that interferes with thinking and memory.

depression: feelings of sadness that last for a long time.

developer: a person who builds or designs things.

device: a piece of equipment meant to do certain things, such as a phone.

discrimination: the unfair treatment of a person or a group of people because of their identity.

distinguished: important.

documentaries: stories about true events.

durable: able to last.

efficiently: wasting as little time or effort as possible when completing a task.

emotion: a strong feeling.

engineer: someone who uses science and math to build things.

epilepsy: a brain condition that causes seizures.

ethnic: sharing customs, languages, and beliefs.

feedback: helpful information or criticism given to improve something.

flight simulator: a game that resembles the act of flying a plane.

forensic: applying scientific methods to investigate a crime.

foundation: the basis on which something is supported or built.

fraud: deception.

global: relating to the entire world.

hardware: the physical parts of a computer or other device.

humanities: the study of literature, philosophy, and other arts.

icon: a person or thing that grows to represent a larger idea.

industry: the large-scale production of something.

inequality: differences in opportunity and treatment based on social, ethnic, racial, or economic qualities.

innovation: a new creation or a unique solution to a problem.

intellectual: involving serious thought.

interactive: having a two-way flow of information between a computer and a user.

interconnected: to connect between things.

intimidating: something that is frightening.

isolating: to cause someone to feel alone.

matter: any material or substance that takes up space.

mechanical drawing: drawing done with rulers, scales, compasses, and other tools.

melanin: a pigment occurring in the hair, skin, and eyes of people and animals.

network: a group of interconnected people or things.

obstacle: something that blocks you from what you want to achieve.

pioneer: one of the first to use or apply a new area of knowledge.

potential: something that is possible, or can develop into something real.

practical: something useful and effective in everyday situations.

predominantly: for the most part, or likely.

prevalent: widespread.

process: to perform a series of operations.

program: a set of step-by-step instructions that tells a computer what to do with the information it has to work with.

prophet: someone who can tell the future.

prosthetic: an artificial body part.

racism: negative opinions or treatment of people based on race.

radar: a system that sends out pulses of radio waves that reflect back.

resilient: able to recover quickly from setbacks.

GLOSSARY

role model: someone who is an inspiration.

salary: a regular payment for work.

satellite: a device that orbits the earth to relay communication signals or transmit information.

security: keeping something safe from danger or harm.

setback: a difficulty or disappointment that must be overcome.

sexism: negative opinions or treatment of people based on gender.

society: a group of people with shared laws, traditions, and values.

software: the programs and other operating information used by a computer.

sonar: an instrument that locates objects with sound waves.

statistics: numbers that show facts about a subject.

systemic: affecting the parts of a whole.

technology: the scientific or mechanical tools, methods, and systems used to solve a problem or do work.

telecommute: to work from home.

trustee: a member of a group that oversees a school, hospital, or other institution.

tutor: a teacher, usually hired for just a few students for extra help.

ubiquitous: appearing everywhere.

virtual: something that exists on a computer or a network.

RESOURCES

Websites

- Girls Who Code
  girlswhocode.com
- Black Girls Code
  blackgirlscode.com
- Hour of Code
  hourofcode.com/us
- Code.org
  code.org
- Girls Go Digital!
  girlsgodigital.org
- Emagination Computer Camps
  computercamps.com

Books

- Padua, Sydney. *The Thrilling Adventures of Lovelace and Babbage: The (Mostly) True Story of the First Computer*. Pantheon, 2015.
- Schatz, Kate. *Rad American Women A-Z: Rebels, Trailblazers, and Visionaries Who Shaped Our History . . . and Our Future*. City Lights Publishers, 2015.
- Thimmesh, Catherine. *Girls Think of Everything: Stories of Ingenious Inventions by Women*. HMH Books for Young Readers, 2002.

RESOURCES

INDEX